The Key Facts™ on

Mongolia

Essential Information on Mongolia

By Patrick W. Nee

The Internationalist®
www.internationalist.com

The Internationalist®

International Business, Investment, and Travel

Published by:

The Internationalist Publishing Company

96 Walter Street/ Suite 200

Boston, MA 02131, USA

Tel: 617-354-7722

www.internationalist.com

PN@internationalist.com

Table Of Contents

Chapter 1: Background

The Mongols gained fame in the 13th century when under Chinggis KHAAN they established a huge Eurasian empire through conquest. After his death the empire was divided into several powerful Mongol states, but these broke apart in the 14th century. The Mongols eventually retired to their original steppe homelands and in the late 17th century came under Chinese rule. Mongolia won its independence in 1921 with Soviet backing and a communist regime was installed in 1924. The modern country of Mongolia, however, represents only part of the Mongols' historical homeland; more ethnic Mongolians live in the Inner Mongolia Autonomous Region in the People's Republic of China than in Mongolia. Following a peaceful democratic revolution, the ex-communist Mongolian People's Revolutionary Party (MPRP) won elections in 1990 and 1992, but was defeated by the Democratic Union Coalition (DUC) in the 1996 parliamentary election. The MPRP won an overwhelming majority in the 2000 parliamentary election, but the party lost seats in the 2004 election and shared power with democratic coalition parties from 2004-08. The MPRP regained a solid majority in the 2008 parliamentary elections but nevertheless formed a coalition government with the Democratic Party that lasted until January 2012.

In 2009, current President ELBEGDORJ of the Democratic Party was elected to office and was re-elected for his second term in June 2013. In 2010, the MPRP voted to retake the name of the Mongolian People's Party (MPP), a name it used in the early 1920s. Shortly thereafter, a new party was formed by former president ENKHBAYAR, which adopted the MPRP name. In the 2012 Parliamentary elections, a coalition of four political parties led by the Democratic Party, gained control of the Parliament.

Chapter 2: Geography

Location:

Northern Asia, between China and Russia

Geographic coordinates:

46 00 N, 105 00 E

Map references:

Asia

Area:

total: 1,564,116 sq km

country comparison to the world: 19

land: 1,553,556 sq km

water: 10,560 sq km

Area - comparative:

slightly smaller than Alaska

Land boundaries:

total: 8,220 km

border countries: China 4,677 km, Russia 3,543 km

Coastline:

0 km (landlocked)

Maritime claims:

none (landlocked)

Climate:

desert; continental (large daily and seasonal temperature ranges)

Terrain:

vast semidesert and desert plains, grassy steppe, mountains in west and southwest; Gobi Desert in south-central

Elevation extremes:

lowest point: Hoh Nuur 560 m

highest point: Nayramadlin Orgil (Huyten Orgil) 4,374 m

Natural resources:

oil, coal, copper, molybdenum, tungsten, phosphates, tin, nickel, zinc, fluorspar, gold, silver, iron

Land use:

arable land: 0.39%

permanent crops: 0%

other: 99.61% (2011)

Irrigated land:

843 sq km (2003)

Total renewable water resources:

34.8 cu km (2011)

Freshwater withdrawal (domestic/industrial/agricultural):

total: 0.55 cu km/yr (13%/43%/44%)

per capita: 196.8 cu m/yr (2009)

Natural hazards:

dust storms; grassland and forest fires; drought; "zud," which is harsh winter conditions

Environment - current issues:

limited natural freshwater resources in some areas; the policies of former Communist regimes promoted rapid urbanization and industrial growth that had negative effects on the environment; the burning of soft coal in power plants and the lack of enforcement of environmental laws severely polluted the air in Ulaanbaatar; deforestation, overgrazing, and the converting of virgin land to agricultural production increased soil erosion from wind and rain; desertification and mining activities had a deleterious effect on the environment

Environment - international agreements:

party to: Biodiversity, Climate Change, Climate Change-Kyoto Protocol, Desertification, Endangered Species, Environmental Modification, Hazardous Wastes, Law of the Sea, Ozone Layer Protection, Ship Pollution, Wetlands, Whaling

signed, but not ratified: none of the selected agreements

Geography - note:

landlocked; strategic location between China and Russia

Chapter 3: People and Society

Nationality:

noun: Mongolian(s)

adjective: Mongolian

Ethnic groups:

Khalkh 81.9%, Kazak 3.8%, Dorvod 2.7%, Bayad 2.1%,

Buryat-Bouriates 1.7%, Zakhchin 1.2%, Dariganga 1%,

Uriankhai 1%, other 4.6% (2010 est.)

Languages:

Khalkha Mongol 90% (official), Turkic, Russian (1999)

Religions:

Buddhist 53%, Muslim 3%, Christian 2.2%, Shamanist

2.9%, other 0.4%, none 38.6% (2010 est.)

Population:

2,953,190 (July 2014 est.)

country comparison to the world: 139

Age structure:

0-14 years: 26.8% (male 404,051/female 388,546)

15-24 years: 18.7% (male 278,912/female 273,167)

25-54 years: 44.5% (male 636,799/female 677,236)

55-64 years: 4.1% (male 80,267/female 94,021)

65 years and over: 4% (male 49,314/female 70,877) (2014

est.)

Dependency ratios:

    total dependency ratio: 45.1 %

    youth dependency ratio: 39.6 %

    elderly dependency ratio: 5.5 %

    potential support ratio: 18.1 (2013)

Median age:

    total: 27.1 years

    male: 26.3 years

    female: 27.8 years (2014 est.)

Population growth rate:

    1.37% (2014 est.)

    country comparison to the world: 89

Birth rate:

    20.88 births/1,000 population (2014 est.)

    country comparison to the world: 81

Death rate:

    6.38 deaths/1,000 population (2014 est.)

    country comparison to the world: 156

Net migration rate:

    -0.85 migrant(s)/1,000 population (2014 est.)

    country comparison to the world: 145

Urbanization:

    urban population: 68.5% of total population (2011)

    rate of urbanization: 2.81% annual rate of change (2010-15 est.)

Major urban areas - population:

ULAANBAATAR (capital) 949,000 (2009)

Sex ratio:

at birth: 1.05 male(s)/female

0-14 years: 1.04 male(s)/female

15-24 years: 1.02 male(s)/female

25-54 years: 0.94 male(s)/female

55-64 years: 0.96 male(s)/female

65 years and over: 0.77 male(s)/female

total population: 1 male(s)/female (2014 est.)

Maternal mortality rate:

63 deaths/100,000 live births (2010)

country comparison to the world: 96

Infant mortality rate:

total: 23.15 deaths/1,000 live births

country comparison to the world: 79

male: 26.4 deaths/1,000 live births

female: 19.75 deaths/1,000 live births (2014 est.)

Life expectancy at birth:

total population: 68.98 years

country comparison to the world: 158

male: 64.72 years

female: 73.45 years (2014 est.)

Total fertility rate:

2.22 children born/woman (2014 est.)

country comparison to the world: 100

Contraceptive prevalence rate:

55% (2010)

Health expenditures:

5.3% of GDP (2011)

country comparison to the world: 129

Physicians density:

2.76 physicians/1,000 population (2008)

Hospital bed density:

6.8 beds/1,000 population (2011)

Drinking water source:

improved:

urban: 100% of population

rural: 53.1% of population

total: 85.3% of population

unimproved:

urban: 0% of population

rural: 46.9% of population

total: 14.7% of population (2011 est.)

Sanitation facility access:

improved:

urban: 64% of population

rural: 29.1% of population

total: 53% of population

unimproved:

    urban: 36% of population

    rural: 70.9% of population

    total: 47% of population (2011 est.)

HIV/AIDS - adult prevalence rate:

less than 0.1% (2009 est.)

country comparison to the world: 161

HIV/AIDS - people living with HIV/AIDS:

fewer than 500 (2009 est.)

country comparison to the world: 160

HIV/AIDS - deaths:

fewer than 100 (2009 est.)

country comparison to the world: 140

Obesity - adult prevalence rate:

14.4% (2008)

country comparison to the world: 122

Children under the age of 5 underweight:

5.3% (2005)

country comparison to the world: 88

Education expenditures:

5.5% of GDP (2011)

country comparison to the world: 58

Literacy:

    <u>definition</u>: age 15 and over can read and write

    <u>total population</u>: 97.4%

    <u>male</u>: 96.8%

    <u>female</u>: 97.9% (2011 est.)

School life expectancy (primary to tertiary education):

    <u>total</u>: 15 years

    <u>male</u>: 14 years

    <u>female</u>: 16 years (2012)

Child labor – children ages 5-14:

    <u>total number:</u> 106,203

    <u>percentage:</u> 18 % (2005 est.)

Unemployment, youth ages 15-24:

    <u>total</u>: 11.9%

    <u>country comparison to the world</u>: 100

    <u>male</u>: 10.7%

    <u>female</u>: 13.2% (2011)

Chapter 4: Government and Key Leaders

Country name:

> conventional long form: none
>
> conventional short form: Mongolia
>
> local long form: none
>
> local short form: Mongol Uls
>
> former: Outer Mongolia

Government type:

> parliamentary

Capital:

> name: Ulaanbaatar
>
> geographic coordinates: 47 55 N, 106 55 E
>
> time difference: UTC+8 (13 hours ahead of Washington, DC during Standard Time)

Administrative divisions:

> 21 provinces (aymguud, singular - aymag) and 1 municipality* (singular - hot); Arhangay, Bayanhongor, Bayan-Olgiy, Bulgan, Darhan-Uul, Dornod, Dornogovi, Dundgovi, Dzavhan (Zavkhan), Govi-Altay, Govisumber, Hentiy, Hovd, Hovsgol, Omnogovi, Orhon, Ovorhangay, Selenge, Suhbaatar, Tov, Ulaanbaatar*, Uvs

Independence:

> 11 July 1921 (from China)

National holiday:

> Independence Day/Revolution Day, 11 July (1921)

Constitution:

several previous; latest adopted 13 January 1992, effective 12 February 1992; amended 1999, 2001 (2011)

Legal system:

civil law system influenced by Soviet and Romano-Germanic legal systems; constitution ambiguous on judicial review of legislative acts

International law organization participation:

has not submitted an ICJ jurisdiction declaration; accepts ICCt jurisdiction

Suffrage:

18 years of age; universal

Executive branch:

chief of state: President Tsakhia ELBEGDORJ (since 18 June 2009)

head of government: Prime Minister Norov ALTANKHUYAG (since 9 August 2012); Deputy Prime Minister Dendev TERBISHDAGVA (since 20 August 2012)

cabinet: Cabinet nominated by the prime minister in consultation with the president and confirmed by the State Great Hural (parliament)

elections: presidential candidates nominated by political parties represented in State Great Hural and elected by popular vote for a four-year term (eligible for a second term); election last held on 26 June 2013 (next to be held in June 2017); following legislative elections, leaders of the majority party or a majority coalition usually elect the prime minister of the State Great Hural

election results: in elections in June 2013, Tsakhia ELBEGDORJ elected president; percent of vote - Tsakhia ELBEGDORJ 50.2%, Badmaanyambuu BAT-ERDENE 42%, Natsag UDVAL 6.5%, others 1.3%

Legislative branch:

unicameral State Great Hural (76 seats; of which 48 members are directly elected from 26 electoral districts, while 28 members are proportionally elected based on a party's share of the total votes; all serve four-year terms)

elections: last held on 28 June 2012 (next to be held in June 2016)

election results: percent of vote by party - NA; seats by party - DP 33, MPP 25, Justice Coalition 11, others 5, vacant 2

Judicial branch:

Highest court(s): Supreme Court (consists of the Chief Justice and 16 judges organized into civil, criminal, and administrative chambers); Constitutional Court or Tsets (consists of a chairman and 8 members)

Judge selection and term of offfice: Supreme Court chief justice and judges appointed by the president upon recommendation to the State Great Hural by the General Council of Courts; term of appointment is for life;

chairman of the Constitutional Court elected from among its members; members appointed by the State Great Heral upon nominations - 3 each by the president, the State Great Hural, and the Supreme Court; term of appointment is 6 years; chairmanship limited to a single renewable 3-year term

subordinate courts: aimag (provincial) and capital city appellate courts; soum, inter-soum, and district courts; Administrative Cases Courts (established in 2004)

Political parties and leaders:

Civil Will-Green Party or CWGP [Sanjaasuren OYUN]

Democratic Party or DP [Norov ALTANHUYAG]

Justice Coalition (includes MPRP and MNDP)

Mongolian National Democratic Party or MNDP [Mendsaikhan ENKHSAIKHAN]

Mongolian People's Party or MPP [Miyegombo ENKHBOLD]

Mongolian People's Revolutionary Party or MPRP [Nambar ENKHBAYAR]

Political pressure groups and leaders:

other: human rights groups; women's groups

International organization participation:

ADB, ARF, CD, CICA, CP, EBRD, EITI (compliant country), FAO, G-77, IAEA, IBRD, ICAO, ICC (NGOs), ICRM, IDA, IFAD, IFC, IFRCS, ILO, IMF, IMO, IMSO, Interpol, IOC, IOM, IPU, ISO, ITSO, ITU, ITUC, MIGA, MINURSO, MONUSCO, NAM, OPCW, OSCE, SCO (observer), UN, UNAMID, UNCTAD, UNESCO, UNIDO, UNISFA, UNMISS, UNWTO, UPU, WCO, WHO, WIPO, WMO, WTO

Diplomatic representation in the US:

chief of mission: Ambassador Bulgaa ALTANGEREL (since 8 January 2013)

chancery: 2833 M Street NW, Washington, DC 20007

telephone: [1] (202) 333-7117

FAX: [1] (202) 298-9227

consulate(s) general: New York, San Francisco

Diplomatic representation from the US:

chief of mission: Ambassador Piper Anne Wind CAMPBELL (since 6 August 2012)

embassy: Denver Street #3, 11th Micro Region, Big Ring Road, Ulaanbaatar, 14190 Mongolia

mailing address: PSC 461, Box 300, FPO AP 96521-0002; P.O. Box 341, Ulaanbaatar-14192

telephone: [976] 7007-6001

FAX: [976] 7007-6016

Key Leaders:

Pres.	Tsakhia ELBEGDORJ
Prime Min.	Norov ALTANKHUYAG
Dep. Prime Min.	Dendev TERBISHDAGVA
Min. of Construction & Urban Development	Tsevelmaa BAYARSAIKHAN
Min. of Culture, Sports, & Tourism	Tsedevdamba OYUNGEREL
Min. of Defense	Dashdemberal BAT-ERDENE
Min. of Economic Development	Nyamjav BATBAYAR
Min. of Education & Science	Luvsannyam GANTMUR
Min. of Energy	Mishig SONOMPIL
Min. of Environment	Sambuu DEMBEREL
Min. of Finance	Mendsaikhan ENKHSAIKHAN
Min. of Food, Agriculture, & Light Industry	Khaltmaa BATTULGA
Min. of Foreign Affairs & Trade	Luvsanvandan BOLD
Min. of Health	Natsag UDVAL
Min. of Justice & Home Affairs	Khishigdemberel TEMUUJIN
Min. of Labor	Yadamsuren SANJMYATAV
Min. of Mining	Davaajav GANKHUYAG
Min. for Population Development & Social Welfare	Sodnomzundui ERDENE
Min. of Road & Transportation	Amarjargal GANSUKH
Min. & Chief of the Govt. Secretariat	Chimed SAIKHANBILEG
Governor, Bank of Mongolia	Naidansuren ZOLJARGAL
Ambassador to the US	Bulgaa ALTANGEREL
Permanent Representative to the UN, New York	Od OCH

Flag description:

three equal, vertical bands of red (hoist side), blue, and red; centered on the hoist-side red band in yellow is the national emblem ("soyombo" - a columnar arrangement of abstract and geometric representation for fire, sun, moon, earth, water, and the yin-yang symbol); blue represents the sky, red symbolizes progress and prosperity

National symbol(s):

soyombo emblem

National anthem:

name: "Mongol ulsyn toriin duulal" (National Anthem of Mongolia)

lyrics/music: Tsendiin DAMDINSUREN/Bilegiin DAMDINSUREN and Luvsanjamts MURJORJ

note: music adopted 1950, lyrics adopted 2006; the anthem's lyrics have been altered on numerous occasions

Chapter 5: Economy

Economy - overview:

Mongolia's extensive mineral deposits and attendant growth in mining-sector activities have transformed Mongolia's economy, which traditionally has been dependent on herding and agriculture. Mongolia's copper, gold, coal, molybdenum, fluorspar, uranium, tin, and tungsten deposits, among others, have attracted foreign direct investment. Soviet assistance, at its height one-third of GDP, disappeared almost overnight in 1990 and 1991 at the time of the dismantlement of the USSR. The following decade saw Mongolia endure both deep recession, because of political inaction and natural disasters, as well as economic growth, because of reform-embracing, free-market economics and extensive privatization of the formerly state-run economy. The country opened a fledgling stock exchange in 1991. Mongolia joined the World Trade Organization in 1997 and seeks to expand its participation in regional economic and trade regimes. Growth averaged nearly 9% per year in 2004-08 largely because of high copper prices globally and new gold production. By late 2008, Mongolia was hit hard by the global financial crisis. Slower global economic growth hurt the country's exports, notably copper, and slashed government revenues. As a result, Mongolia's real economy contracted 1.3% in 2009. In early 2009, the International Monetary Fund reached a $236 million Stand-by Arrangement with Mongolia and the country has largely emerged from the crisis with better regulations and closer supervision. The banking sector strengthened but weaknesses remain. In October 2009, Mongolia passed long-awaited legislation on an investment agreement to develop the Oyu Tolgoi mine, considered to be among the world's largest untapped copper-gold deposits. Mongolia's ongoing dispute with a foreign investor over Oyu Tolgoi, however, has called into question the attractiveness of Mongolia as a destination for foreign direct investment. Negotiations to develop the massive Tavan Tolgoi coal field also have stalled. The economy has grown more than 10% per year since 2010, largely on the strength of commodity exports to nearby countries and high government spending domestically. Mongolia's economy, however, faces near-term economic risks from the government's loose fiscal and monetary policies, which are contributing to high inflation, and from uncertainties in foreign demand for Mongolian exports. Trade with China represents more than half of Mongolia's total external trade - China receives more than 90% of Mongolia's exports and is Mongolia's largest supplier. Mongolia has relied on Russia for energy supplies, leaving it vulnerable to price increases; in the first 11 months of 2013, Mongolia purchased 76% of its gasoline and diesel fuel and a substantial amount of electric power from Russia. A drop in foreign direct investment and a decrease in Chinese demand for Mongolia's mineral exports are putting pressure on Mongolia's balance of payments. Remittances from Mongolians working abroad, particularly in South Korea, are significant.

GDP (purchasing power parity):

$17.03 billion (2013 est.)

country comparison to the world: 140

$15.23 billion (2012 est.)

$13.57 billion (2011 est.)

note: data are in 2013 US dollars

GDP (official exchange rate):

$11.14 billion (2013 est.)

GDP - real growth rate:

11.8% (2013 est.)

country comparison to the world: 5

12.3% (2012 est.)

17.5% (2011 est.)

GDP - per capita (PPP):

$5,900 (2013 est.)

country comparison to the world: 152

$5,400 (2012 est.)

$4,900 (2011 est.)

note: data are in 2013 US dollars

GDP – composition, by end use:

household consumption: 58.5%

government consumption: 14.9%

investment in fixed capital: 55.8%

investment in inventories: 0%

exports of goods and services: 50%

imports of goods and services: -79.2% (2013 est.)

GDP - composition by sector:

agriculture: 16.5%

industry: 32.6%

services: 50.9% (2013 est.)

Agriculture – products:

wheat, barley, vegetables, forage crops; sheep, goats, cattle, camels, horses

Industries:

construction and construction materials; mining (coal, copper, molybdenum, fluorspar, tin, tungsten, and gold); oil; food and beverages; processing of animal products, cashmere and natural fiber manufacturing

Industrial production growth rate:

11% (2013 est.)

country comparison to the world: 10

Labor force:

1.037 million (2011 est.)

country comparison to the world: 141

Labor force - by occupation:

agriculture: 33%

industry: 10.6%

services: 56.4% (2011)

Unemployment rate:

9% (2011 est.)

country comparison to the world: 99

13% (2010)

Population below poverty line:

29.8% (2011 est.)

Household income or consumption by percentage share:

lowest 10%: 3%

highest 10%: 28.4% (2008)

Distribution of family income - Gini index:

36.5 (2008)

country comparison to the world: 84

32.8 (2002)

Budget:

revenues: $3.462 billion

expenditures: $4.36 billion (2013 est.)

Taxes and other revenues:

31.1% of GDP (2013 est.)

country comparison to the world: 86

Budget surplus (+) or deficit (-):

-8.1% of GDP (2013 est.)

country comparison to the world: 197

Inflation rate (consumer prices):

8.2% (2013 est.)

country comparison to the world: 195

15% (2012 est.)

Central bank discount rate:

13.25% (31 December 2012)

country comparison to the world: 15

12.25% (31 December 2011 est.)

Commercial bank prime lending rate:

17.5% (31 December 2013 est.)

country comparison to the world: 25

18.2% (31 December 2012 est.)

Stock of narrow money:

$1.219 billion (31 December 2013 est.)

country comparison to the world: 144

$1.318 billion (31 December 2012 est.)

Stock of broad money:

$6.329 billion (31 December 2013 est.)

country comparison to the world: 120

$5.472 billion (31 December 2012 est.)

Stock of domestic credit:

$3.297 billion (31 December 2013 est.)

country comparison to the world: 124

$3.09 billion (31 December 2012 est.)

Market value of publicly traded shares:

$1.293 billion (31 December 2012 est.)

country comparison to the world: 100

$1.579 billion (31 December 2011)

$1.093 billion (31 December 2010 est.)

Current account balance:

-$3.639 billion (2013 est.)

country comparison to the world: 162

-$3.362 billion (2012 est.)

Exports:

$4.294 billion (2013 est.)

country comparison to the world: 116

$4.382 billion (2012 est.)

Exports - commodities:

copper, apparel, livestock, animal products, cashmere, wool, hides, fluorspar, other nonferrous metals, coal, crude oil

Exports - partners:

China 89%, Canada 4.1% (2012)

Imports:

$5.696 billion (2013 est.)

country comparison to the world: 121

$5.934 billion (2012 est.)

Imports - commodities:

machinery and equipment, fuel, cars, food products, industrial consumer goods, chemicals, building materials, cigarettes and tobacco, appliances, soap and detergent

Imports - partners:

China 37.5%, Russia 25.6%, US 9.4%, South Korea 6.1%, Japan 4.9% (2012)

Debt - external:

$4.954 billion (31 December 2013 est.)

country comparison to the world: 122

$4.669 billion (31 December 2012 est.)

Stock of direct foreign investment – at home:

$1.69 billion (31 December 2013 est.)

country comparison to the world: 99

$4.452 billion (31 December 2012 est.)

Stock of direct foreign investment – abroad:

$NA (31 December 2013 est.)

$44 million (31 December 2012 est.)

Exchange rates:

togrog/tugriks (MNT) per US dollar -

1,444.3 (2013 est.)

1,357.6 (2012 est.)

1,357.1 (2010 est.)

1,442.8 (2009)

1,170 (2007)

Chapter 6: Energy

Electricity - production:

4.48 billion kWh (2010 est.)

country comparison to the world: 120

Electricity - consumption:

3.951 billion kWh (2010 est.)

country comparison to the world: 123

Electricity - exports:

22 million kWh (2010 est.)

country comparison to the world: 88

Electricity - imports:

263 million kWh (2010 est.)

country comparison to the world: 82

Electricity - installed generating capacity:

833,200 kW (2010 est.)

country comparison to the world: 127

Electricity - from fossil fuels:

99.9% of total installed capacity (2010 est.)

country comparison to the world: 44

Electricity - from nuclear fuels:

0% of total installed capacity (2010 est.)

country comparison to the world: 133

Electricity - from hydroelectric plants:

0% of total installed capacity (2010 est.)

country comparison to the world: 182

Electricity - from other renewable sources:

0.1% of total installed capacity (2010 est.)

country comparison to the world: 102

Crude oil - production:

9,935 bbl/day (2012 est.)

country comparison to the world: 91

Crude oil - exports:

5,680 bbl/day (2010 est.)

country comparison to the world: 64

Crude oil - imports:

0 bbl/day (2010 est.)

country comparison to the world: 88

Refined petroleum products - production:

0 bbl/day (2010 est.)

country comparison to the world: 169

Refined petroleum products - consumption:

21,610 bbl/day (2011 est.)

country comparison to the world: 125

Refined petroleum products - exports:

0 bbl/day (2010 est.)

country comparison to the world: 194

Refined petroleum products - imports:

17,360 bbl/day (2010 est.)

country comparison to the world: 109

Natural gas - production:

0 cu m (2011 est.)

country comparison to the world: 161

Natural gas - consumption:

0 cu m (2010 est.)

country comparison to the world: 167

Natural gas - exports:

0 cu m (2011 est.)

country comparison to the world: 142

Natural gas - imports:

0 cu m (2011 est.)

country comparison to the world: 92

Natural gas - proved reserves:

0 cu m (1 January 2013 es)

country comparison to the world: 165

Carbon dioxide emissions from consumption of energy:

10.21 million Mt (2011 est.)

country comparison to the world: 100

Chapter 7: Communications

Telephones - main lines in use:

176,700 (2012)

country comparison to the world: 129

Telephones - mobile cellular:

3.375 million (2012)

country comparison to the world: 126

Telephone system:

general assessment: network is improving with international direct dialing available in many areas; a fiber-optic network has been installed that is improving broadband and communication services between major urban centers with multiple companies providing inter-city fiber-optic cable services

domestic: very low fixed-line teledensity; there are multiple mobile-cellular providers and subscribership is increasing

international: country code - 976; satellite earth stations - 7 (2011)

Broadcast media:

following a law passed in 2005, Mongolia's state-run radio and TV provider converted to a public service provider; also available are private radio and TV broadcasters, as well as multi-channel satellite and cable TV providers; more than 100 radio stations, including some 20 via

repeaters for the public broadcaster; transmissions of
multiple international broadcasters are available (2008)

Internet country code:

.kh.mn

Internet hosts:

20,084 (2012)

country comparison to the world: 118

Internet users:

330,000 (2008)

country comparison to the world: 125

Chapter 8: Transportation

Airports:

    44 (2013)

    country comparison to the world: 98

Airports - with paved runways:

    total: 15

    over 3,057 m: 2

    2,438 to 3,047 m: 10

    1,524 to 2,437 m: 3 (2013)

Airports - with unpaved runways:

    total: 29

    over 3,047 m: 2

    2,438 to 3,047 m: 2

    1,524 to 2,437 m: 24

    under 914 m: 1 (2013)

Heliports:

    1 (2013)

Railways:

    total: 1,908 km

    country comparison to the world: 73

    broad gauge: 1,908 km 1.520-m gauge

    note: the railway is 50 percent owned by the Russian State Railway (2010)

Roadways:

> total: 49,249 km

> country comparison to the world: 78

> paved: 4,800 km

> unpaved: 44,449 km (2013)

Waterways:

> 580 km (the only waterway in operation is Lake Hovsgol) (135 km); Selenge River (270 km) and Orhon River (175 km) are navigable but carry little traffic; lakes and rivers freeze in winter, they are open from May to September) (2010)

> country comparison to the world: 82

Merchant marine:

> total: 57

> country comparison to the world: 68

> by type: bulk carrier 21, cargo 25, chemical tanker 1, container 2, liquefied gas 2, passenger/cargo 2, roll on/roll off 3, vehicle carrier 1

> foreign-owned: 44 (Indonesia 2, Japan 2, North Korea 1, Russia 2, Singapore 3, Ukraine 1, Vietnam 33) (2010)

Chapter 9: Military

Military branches:

> Mongolian Armed Forces (Mongol ulsyn zevsegt huchin): Mongolian Army (includes Mongolian Air and Air Defense, which is to become a separate service in 2015); there is no navy (2013)

Military service age and obligation:

> 18-25 years of age for compulsory and voluntary military service; conscript service obligation is 12 months in land or air defense forces or police; a small portion of Mongolian land forces (2.5 percent) is comprised of contract soldiers; women cannot be deployed overseas for military operations (2012)

Manpower available for military service:

> males age 16-49: 898,546
>
> females age 16-49: 891,192 (2010 est.)

Manpower fit for military service:

> males age 16-49: 726,199
>
> females age 16-49: 756,628 (2010 est.)

Manpower reaching militarily significant age annually:

> male: 30,829
>
> female: 29,648 (2010 est.)

Military expenditures:

1.12% of GDP (2012)

country comparison to the world: 92

0.99% of GDP (2011)

1.12% of GDP (2010)

Chapter 10: Transnational Issues

Disputes - international:

Refugees and internally displaced persons:

stateless persons: 220 (2012)

Map of Mongolia

Other Key Facts™ Titles

Key Facts on Syria

Key Facts on China

Key Facts on Qatar

Key Facts on India

Key Facts on Germany

Key Facts on Argentina

Key Facts on Russia

Key Facts on North Korea

Key Facts on Brazil

Key Facts on Italy

Key Facts on the United Arab Emirates

Key Facts on the European Union

Key Facts on Pakistan

Key Facts on Saudi Arabia

Key Facts on Cyprus

Key Facts on Iran

Key Facts on Afghanistan

Key Facts on Iraq

Key Facts on Indonesia

Key Facts on South Korea

Key Facts on France

Key Facts on the United Kingdom

Key Facts on Egypt

Key Facts on Israel

All Key Facts™ Titles are Available at

www.Amazon.com

THE INTERNATIONALIST®

2014

WWW.INTERNATIONALIST.COM